C000198834

WESTON-SUPER-MARE
A Pictorial History

WESTON-SUPER-MARE
THE SMILE IN SMILING SOMERSET
Guide free from A. R. Turner, Town Hall, Weston-super-Mare
TRAVEL BY TRAIN

Publicity poster for Weston-super-Mare, 1959.

WESTON-SUPER-MARE
A Pictorial History

Sharon Poole
Woodspring Museum Service

Phillimore

1995

Published by
PHILLIMORE & CO. LTD.
Shopwyke Manor Barn, Chichester, West Sussex

© Woodspring Museum Service, 1995

ISBN 0 85033 969 3

Printed and bound in Great Britain by
BIDDLES LTD.
Guildford, Surrey

List of Illustrations

Acknowledgements

Woodspring Museum Service wishes to thank all those who have donated photographs and postcards to the Museum over the years. Every photograph, however apparently trivial, helps to build up a picture of the development of Weston-super-Mare since the birth of photography. Without this record our knowledge of the town would be that much the poorer. The Museum Service also acknowledges the invaluable work of the late E.C. Amesbury. For nearly 30 years, Ted Amesbury copied original photographs and produced prints for display, publication and other uses.

Specifically we would like to thank the following for illustrations: Mr. K. Durston, 80; Mr. L. Trowbridge, 105; Mr. Barnett, 117; Mr. M. Davies, 143.

If you are able to tell us more about the pictures in this book, or have photographs or postcards you would be willing to donate or lend to the Museum Service, please contact Woodspring Museum Service, Burlington Street, Weston-super-Mare, BS23 1PR or telephone them on (01934) 621028.

Introduction

Farewell to thee Weston; I loved thee before,
And each visit I pay thee endears thee yet more;
So healing, so bracing, so pure is thy air,
Can any inhale and its virtues not share?
So varied thy walks, so extensive thy beach,
Old and young, sick and healthful, thou'rt suited to each.

The above poem was a view of visitors to Weston-super-Mare in the 19th century. A century which saw Weston grow from a tiny village of about one hundred inhabitants to a thriving Victorian seaside resort of nearly 20,000 people; from a scattering of a few thatched cottages to the promenades, piers, hotels and boarding houses of a flourishing seaside resort.

Despite inevitable comparisons, the only thing most seaside resorts have in common is the sea! The development of every resort has been influenced by different factors and, as a result, each has a character of its own. Weston's character was formed during the 19th century by men of vision—entrepreneurs whose bold decisions turned Weston-super-Mare into the town it is today.

The name Weston is made up of two Old English or Saxon words meaning the west *tun* or settlement. There were at least ten different places called Weston in Somerset, so, by the 13th century, descriptions were added to tell them apart. Thus we have North Weston and Weston in Gordano. What is distinctive about Weston-super-Mare is that the descriptive part of its name has remained in medieval Latin. *Super* (with small 's') is a Latin preposition meaning on or above, and *mare* is Latin for sea. Other towns have anglicised their names over the centuries, such as Burnham-on-Sea.

Earliest Times

Though Weston is mainly thought of as a Victorian resort, its beginnings go back thousands of years. On Worlebury Hill, which dominates the town on its northern side, the remains of a prehistoric site, known as Worlebury hillfort, may still be seen. This ancient stronghold was built over 2,000 years ago, in the Iron Age, and consists of massive stone ramparts which enclose the western end of the hill. A great deal about the hillfort was revealed during excavations in the 1850s, including the presence of many large and deep pits cut into the underlying rock. These pits were probably used for storage, particularly for grain. Some were later re-used, however, for burying people and these human remains, some of which show evidence of a violent death with sword cut-marks, are the most famous finds from Worlebury.

As the town was developed it soon became apparent that ancient remains were not only to be found in the hillfort. Local newspapers frequently contained details of discoveries such as Iron-Age and Roman pottery, animal bones and quite often human skeletons. What was being revealed by the Victorian builders was evidence of a sprawling settlement which spread down and along from the area of the hillfort, on the southern flank of the hill.

Even older remains were being discovered in the surrounding quarries that provided much of the stone that was used to build the town. Bones of animals, such as hyena, woolly rhinoceros and mammoth were found, and at Milton the teeth of an extinct type of rhinoceros were uncovered which are now known to be around 120,000 years old.

Village Weston

For a few hundred years from the time the Romans left in the fifth century B.C., Weston existed as a small community of people depending on farming and fishing for their living. Weston itself is not mentioned in Domesday Book, the closest manor being that of Ashcombe, now only surviving as the name of a park and in road names. The church was the centre of village life and, although we do not know exactly when it was built, it is known to have been a parish church by 1226, the year of the first written reference to Weston. This occurred in the registers of the Dean and Chapter of Wells. Cottages straggled along the line of what is now the High Street, then bounded by a stream and withy beds. Before the promenade was built in the 19th century, the beach stretched much further inland and sand formed dunes as far as what are now Regent and Meadow Streets. The hillside was used as open grazing land. It had no trees at that time and would have looked much as Brean Down and Sand Point do today.

Queen Elizabeth I was anxious to develop a metal industry in England and at that time the Germans led the world in metallurgy and so it was they who were commissioned to survey the country in search of ores. In 1568, deposits of calamine were discovered by German miners on Worle Hill. This type of zinc ore was very important in the production of brass. It was a significant moment in the history of Weston, and the village must have been a hive of activity. Calamine continued to be mined locally well into the 19th century.

Another ore abundant in Worlebury Hill was galena, a lead ore. The hummocky 'gruffy-ground' resulting from the workings is still evident in Weston Woods, and also above Milton and Worle. Judging from the discovery of a hoard of lead-ore fragments buried in one of the ditches of the hillfort in the woods, lead-mining possibly dates back to Iron-Age times.

By 1600 Weston had its own manor, held at that time by William Arthur of Clapton. It then passed by marriage to the Winter family who held it until 1696 when the estate was sold to John Pigott. The Pigotts, and later the Smyth-Pigotts, continued to hold the manor until the estate was sold off in 1914. The main seat of the Pigotts was at Brockley, but they built a summer holiday cottage in The Grove. This wooded copse, now Grove Park, was situated close to the old rectory and parish church on the slope above the marshy lowland. In 1791, encouraged by the proximity of suitable neighbours at The Grove, the Rev. Leeves of Wrington built his own seaside cottage on the dunes. A fragment of this cottage survives as *The Old Thatched Cottage Restaurant*. This, together with Glebe House, once the rectory, are all that remain today of the village of Weston.

Glebe House dates to the 17th century. In 1644, during the English Civil War, the royalist rector, Christopher Sadbury, imprisoned rebel villagers in the house. The house has been enlarged and altered over the years but many original features can still be traced.

In 1815 the Weston Enclosure Award was completed. This defined certain paths and roads and established ownership of land. It was this Award, together with plentiful local supplies of building materials and the increasing belief of the medicinal value of the Sea Cure, which set Weston on the path of development.

An Early Seaside Resort

By the middle of the 18th century, doctors in London and elsewhere started to prescribe courses of sea-water drinking and sea bathing for their patients, a new fashion to replace old-established visits to inland spas. The Prince of Wales bathed at Brighton in 1783 and eventually persuaded his father to try it. At Weymouth in 1789, George III took a dip from a royal bathing machine and thereafter everyone in fashionable society wanted to do the same. So the stage was set for doctors in Bath and Bristol to send their patients to suitable parts of the coastline within easy reach of a road.

In 1773 the writer Langhorne stayed at Weston-super-Mare, where he met the philanthropist and reformer, Hannah More, though it is not recorded whether either of them bathed. However, in April and May 1797 an advertisement was placed in the *Bristol Journal:* 'For health and Sea Bathing. At Uphill Jane Biss and Son most respectfully inform the public that they have fitted up two commodious houses for the reception of families or single persons during the summer at reasonable terms.'

At Weston the right of sea bathing and the duty of providing proper means and facilities rested with the lord of the manor. The three Pigott family bathing machines were the first on the beach. Then, in 1808, the squire granted rights to John Baker 'to bathe in every part of the sea within the said Manor of Weston-super-Mare and to use machines for that purpose'.

During the 18th century most people bathed naked. For this reason the sheltered and secluded cove at Anchor Head was chosen as Weston's first bathing place. In 1829 Rutter wrote of Anchor Head in his *Delineations of the County of Somerset* that 'It is inaccessible to machines, but is romantic, secluded, and convenient at all tides, so that ladies frequently resort to it for bathing'. Here bathing attendant Betty Muggleworth spread an old sail between the rocks where ladies changed into coarse shifts before walking down the pebbly beach to the water. Nervous bathers were unceremoniously 'dipped' by Betty. As modesty prevailed the bathing machine was invented. This was a hut on wheels. The bather entered and, as the machine was drawn down to the sea by a horse, they changed into a bathing dress. They were then able to descend the steps directly into the water, unseen from the beach.

By this time the lack of anywhere congenial for visitors to stay was proving a problem. Some local businessmen formed a partnership, resulting in the opening of *The Hotel* in 1810. This is part of what is now the *Royal Hotel*. The laying of the foundation stone was such a momentous event for the village that the West Mendip Militia fired a musket volley in celebration of the occasion.

The idea of a communal medicinal bath house, and the social side that went with it, still persisted, however, from the spa days. In Weston, Knightstone was chosen for this site. In its natural state Knightstone was a barren, rocky island

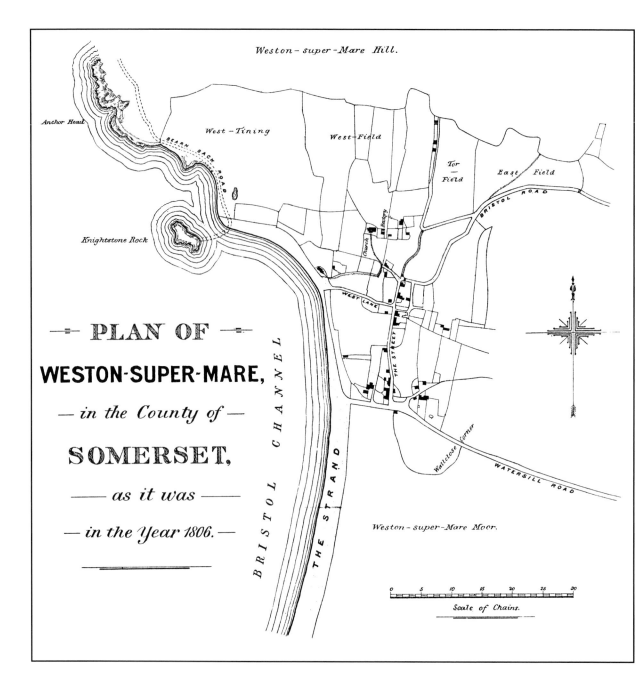

PLAN OF
WESTON-SUPER-MARE,
— in the County of —
SOMERSET,
—— as it was ——
— in the Year 1806. —

Weston – super – Mare Hill.

Anchor Head

West – Tining

West – Field

Tor Field

East Field

BEARN BACK ROAD

BRISTOL ROAD

Knightstone Rock

Vicary

Church

WEST LANE

THE STREET

BRISTOL CHANNEL

THE STRAND

Wattclose Corner

WATERSILL ROAD

Weston – super – Mare Moor.

| 0 | 5 | 10 | 15 | 20 | 25 | 30 |

Scale of Chains.

accessible only at low tide. It was a good fishing spot (a salmon of 30lb was once landed there), and sheltered a small harbour. Since 1696 the island formed part of the Pigott estate but in the early 19th century it was bought by John Howe of Bristol for £200.

Howe's baths opened in July 1820 offering hot and cold salt water baths. A two-storey house was built on the island as lodgings for the invalids; there were also a refreshment room and reading room. The facilities were expensive, however. The cost of a hot bath was three shillings and it was one shilling for a cold bath. As Knightstone was still an island, bathers were ferried over by local boatman, Aaron Fisher. Not until 1824, when the baths were owned by the Rev. Thomas Pruen, was a low causeway built to the island but it was passable only at low tide.

Weston's first guide book for visitors was written in 1822. It paints a vivid portrait of the village at that time. Described as a 'fashionable summer retreat', the town's population was then seven hundred and thirty-five. The language used drew a poetic picture of the expanding village:

> On a fine summer evening nothing can be more beautiful than the scene which it presents; numerous groups walking on its extensive sands, a variety of carriages of all descriptions, horses, ponys [*sic*], donkeys, wheel chairs, etc., fishermen shrimping, and the villagers enjoying the high tide after the labours of the day; whilst the distant coast of Wales, the white sails of the vessels in the harbour of Cardiff, the Steep and Flat Holmes, and the setting sun (which appears particularly fine from this spot, at one period of the year gilding the level line of the horizon, and at others, slowly sinking behind the hills), form a most interesting *coup d'oeil.*

One hotel, two inns and a number of lodging houses catered for visitors. There was a Methodist chapel, in addition to the parish church, and a post office. Weston was described as a 'penny post from Bristol', the letters being brought by carrier every evening from May to November and every Monday, Wednesday and Friday morning during the winter months. There was little organised entertainment—a billiard table, a reading room and two pleasure boats for hire. Visitors would have read, sketched, walked and conversed. Dances would have been held at the Assembly Rooms. There were three public bathing machines available on the sands.

Among the list of facilities mentioned in the 1822 *Guide* was a school room. This was a Sunday School, run by the Rev. Jenkins. Concern had been expressed over the large number of illiterate boys, attracted to the town by the promise of summer work, tending donkeys and the like. These boys were left to fend for themselves during the winter months and so a Sunday School was set up to 'impart to these youths thus thrown adrift upon the world, the advantages of a sound religious education, as the means of regulating their future life and making them moral and useful members of society' (*Weston Gazette*, 15 May 1845).

By 1824 it was apparent that the small Norman parish church was no longer adequate for the increased number of residents and seasonal visitors. It was also in a poor state of repair with straw patching holes in the roof and broken windows. Rather than repair it, it was decided to build a brand new church built on the same site. The next step forward was the building of a promenade. Although this first section only ran from Knightstone to Leeves Cottage, visitors now had a proper place to walk and take in the bracing air.

In September 1830 Dr. Edward Long Fox of Brislington purchased Knightstone. This prominent Quaker physician was a pioneer in the humane treatment of the insane. Sea-bathing was seen as a cure for both physical and mental disorders and Dr. Fox's patients came from both categories. He was assisted in his work by his son, Dr. Francis Ker Fox and much development took place on the island at this time. An exercise courtyard for patients was created and a new elegant baths building erected 'for the purpose of introducing fresh and salt water, hot and cold vapour and shower, sulphur and every description of medicated baths' (*Bristol Mirror*, 11 August 1832). This fine building survives today.

The Railway Arrives

It was the arrival of the railway in 1841 which really speeded up development in all senses. Weston's first station was at the end of a single branch line, where the famous floral clock is now. This left the main Bristol to Exeter railway line at Weston Junction, the trains initially being drawn by horses as the residents were not too keen on having noisy and smelly steam engines in their growing town. Both stations were designed by Isambard K. Brunel. In 1866 a new larger station was built, with a separate goods station nearby. It was, however, still a terminus on a branch line, albeit with a double track.

The coming of the railway opened up country-wide markets for locally-produced goods. One of the first firms to take advantage of this was the Royal Pottery. In the 1840s two businesses were established, both in Locking Road, to produce bricks, tiles and garden ware from the local clay. The firms later amalgamated and became the Royal Pottery. By the 1870s this firm became famous throughout the world for quality garden pottery, from one-inch flower pots to six-foot statues.

Village to Town

Much of the 19th-century development took place under the watchful eye of the lord of the manor. As the largest landowner, he was in a position to dictate the type and density of building that took place, especially on the hillside. The hill-slopes above Weston still bear the marks of limestone quarrying, a distinctive feature of the town being the use of this hard grey, fawn or pinkish stone, for the construction of the older buildings and garden walls. Stone unfit for load-bearing, but of attractive or curious appearance, was kept for decoration, often as 'soldiers' along the tops of walls.

The most important local source of the stone was the Town Quarry, at the top of Queens Road. At other Weston quarries, limestone was burnt in kilns to make lime, a substance particularly important in the building trade for lime-wash, mortar and plaster.

On 13 May 1842 the Improvement and Market Act was granted. This Act brought the first real local government to Weston-super-Mare as until this date different aspects of running the town came under different authorities, among them the Diocese of Bath and Wells, the Churchwardens, the Manor and the Overseers of the Poor.

Eighteen local townsmen put themselves forward to become the First Commissioners, the posts being filled subsequently by public vote. They possessed far-reaching powers to be used for the improvement of the town, and brought in many of the local government controls in existence today. The Improvement Act enabled the Commissioners to levy rates, to borrow money for improvements, to declare paths and streets public highways and to compulsorily purchase property and land for the benefit of the town. The Act makes interesting reading today. From this point no new property was allowed to have a thatched roof, front doors had to open inwards and gutters and down pipes became compulsory so that persons underneath would not get wet from roof water. Bylaws were brought in to control and license hackney cabs, the market, welfare and control of animals and causing a public nuisance; for example, a £2 fine could be levied for bathing in the sea without the use of a machine! The Commissioners also set up Weston's first paid police force.

A Pier is Built

Boats had been offering pleasure trips to and from Weston since the 1820s. These early excursions were often on colliers or coal boats, scrubbed up for the occasion, embarking passengers at Knightstone Harbour. Now the town felt that the time was right to add that most seaside of structures—a pier.

Birnbeck Pier was completed in 1867. Piers were a Victorian invention and, although they can still be seen all around the coast of Britain, Birnbeck is the only one leading to an island.

The thousands of visitors now had further space to walk and take the air. Meanwhile the town grew with villas, estates and boulevards. There were drives and walks through the young trees (now Weston Woods), planted by the lord of the manor in the 1820s as a private game reserve, and from the top it was possible to enjoy splendid vistas as far as Exmoor and Wales.

The 1880s saw further important developments. The Seafront Improvement Scheme was started. This ambitious project resulted in the sea walls and two-mile promenade still in use today. Secondly, Weston finally gained a through railway station when the present station and loop line into the town opened in 1884. The town became a mecca for thousands of visitors, many of them day trippers on Bank Holiday trips and works outings. Weston's heyday had begun.

As the seasonal visitors increased, so the infrastructure grew to cater for them. New shops opened amd the High Street took on the rôle it maintains today. Private schools were set up in Weston-super-Mare throughout the 19th and early 20th centuries, as it became fashionable for the wealthy to send their children to seaside boarding schools. Many of these schools made particular mention in their prospectuses of the healthy air and its benefits for delicate children. The hospital, opened in 1863, was enlarged and social and sporting clubs were formed.

The Early Twentieth Century

Weston began the new century with an Urban District Council, set up in 1894 to replace the old Town Commissioners and Board of Health.

The Edwardians looked for more fun and freedom than previous generations. New facilities to entertain the visitors were built during this period: on Knightstone new indoor swimming baths and a theatre were built; a new library and museum was constructed in the Boulevard; bathing machines disappeared, hastened by the Great Gale of 1903 which wrecked the majority of them; entertainers were everywhere, on the sands, in the parks and pavilions, even on the streets.

The visitors needed somewhere to stay and there was big growth in the number of hotels and boarding houses. One sore point with local traders, however, was the fact that the many thousands of trippers arriving by steamer from Wales never actually got as far as the town centre. There was so much to do on the pier itself. At the turn of the century Birnbeck Pier boasted a theatre of wonders, alpine railway, shooting gallery, park swings, merry go round, tea and coffee rooms, bar, bandstand, photographic studios, switchback, waterchute, flying machine, helter skelter, maze, bioscope, cake walk and zigzag slide. Frequently six or eight steamers would be queuing to disembark passengers and the average August Bank Holiday traffic landed 15,000 people!

It was decided to build another pier, closer to the town centre and, in 1904, the first part of the Grand Pier opened, including the pavilion with its theatre. In order to encourage steamer traffic to call, a further length of 450m was added so that boats could call even at low tide. No-one appeared to take the treacherous currents into consideration, however, and a year later, after several failed attempts, the steamer companies refused to call there.

The Weston-super-Mare tramway was also laid about this time. A fleet of 12 double-deck cars and four cross-bench cars (or toast-rack trams) ran along the seafront from the sanatorium to Birnbeck Pier, and inland along Oxford Street to the depot in Locking Road. This method of transport proved very popular and some passengers travelled two or three times just for the fun of it. There was no timetable—the trams ran according to demand or season. Cabmen and wagonette owners were not so impressed. As they saw much of their business being eroded by the tramways, they operated a campaign of deliberate obstruction. A Court Order had to be obtained to prevent cabs being parked across the tracks or horse brakes being driven slowly in front of a tram.

The First World War

Weston played its part in the First World War. In Weston Woods 80 per cent of the timber was felled for a variety of military uses, the ash being used in the burgeoning aircraft industry. Other wood was used for tent pegs, firewood and shoring trenches. At home some of the timber was used for pit props in the mines. The loss of horses and men to the battlefronts had far reaching effects and Weston had the distinction of having the first female tram drivers in the country. Large numbers of soldiers were billeted in Weston for training prior to being posted, and a Red Cross hospital for the wounded was set up in Ashcombe House.

Town to Borough

The 1920s and '30s saw a lot more development. The Marine Lake was constructed to provide a safe shallow beach where the tide was always in. The Winter Gardens and Pavilion opened in 1927, followed in the 1930s by the Open Air Pool, Odeon cinema and last but not least an airport. At one time it was thought that Weston Airfield would become one of the largest in the country. Weston Airfield was officially opened in June 1936, when air travel was still very much a novelty. Particularly popular was the 10-minute cross-channel service to Wales. Both Weston and Cardiff airports were close to their respective town centres and many South Wales miners flew over to Weston on their days off. Over the 1937 Whitsun holiday, 2,555 passengers travelled on Western Airways from Weston Airport, a world record at that time.

This period was one of much change in transport. The wagonettes and brakes gave way to charabancs which thundered into Weston-super-Mare to the rapturous delight of many a small inland child. Laurie Lee immortalises a day trip for the Slad Choir Outing in his book *Cider with Rosie* when he writes of 'a vast blue sky and an infinity of mud stretching away to the shadows of Wales'. Charabancs in their turn gave way to coaches and, later, private cars. The end of the trams came in 1937 as they were driven out of business by the rise of motor coaches and buses. At one time competition between the two was so fierce that a race would develop to pick up passengers, sometimes resulting in the tram's trolley boom becoming de-wired on corners. Trains were still popular and to accommodate the numbers of visitors a separate excursion station was built in 1914. This was on Locking Road beside the

Odeon cinema and, as the trains disgorged their passengers, crowds would be seen making their way up Regent Street to the beach.

This period culminated in the town being granted Borough Status in 1937. Henry Butt became the first mayor and 'Ever Forward' was chosen for the town's motto on the coat of arms.

The Second World War

Weston was not the quiet backwater that the many evacuees hoped to find when they arrived here from London and other large cities. Because of its aircraft factories and RAF training establishments, Weston suffered several heavy bombing raids.

The first siren warning was sounded on 25 June 1940, but it was not until 14 August that year that the first bombs fell on Weston. The worst blitzes took place in January 1941 and in June 1942. During these raids large areas of the town were devastated. The Tivoli cinema, Boulevard Congregational Church, Grove Park Pavilion, Lance & Lance and Marks & Spencer's were all destroyed. Other damage took place in Oxford Street, Orchard Street, Wadham Street, and Prospect Place as well as residential areas further from the centre.

Because of Weston's position in the south of Britain, the town played its part in the preparations for the Normandy Landings. American troops arrived in the town in October 1943 to equip and train for the invasion. Most of the soldiers were billeted in local hotels and boarding houses. The *Rozel*, the *Grand Atlantic*, *Hotel Villa Rosa* and the *Cairo Hotel* were among those requisitioned for the purpose. Other troops were placed with local families. A large tented encampment was built on Beach Lawns and part of Weston Golf Course was occupied by a US mobile gun battery. Military equipment was stockpiled in the town with Weston Woods used extensively for this purpose. Vehicles were parked on both sides of Worlebury Hill Road and the movement of vehicles towards the woods is marked by a trail of damage still visible today. For example, the wall outside the shop on the corner of Milton Hill and Worlebury Hill Road was partly demolished by a low-loader carrying a tank unable to take the sharp-corner. Some of the equipment arrived in large wooden packing cases. These were eagerly snapped up by local residents for use as garden sheds! One morning in late May 1944 residents awoke to find the soldiers had all left and everyone waited for news of the invasion.

The Post-War Era

At the end of the war, the borough council paused to take stock. Weston had undergone numerous changes, both to the physical fabric of the town and socially. Various proposals aimed at returning Weston to a premier seaside resort and tackling what were seen as the main priorities—housing and transport needs—were considered.

The most controversial plan, was the proposed 'slum clearance' of the Carlton Street area. This large site, covering streets such as Carlton Street, Castle Street, Union Street, New Street, Maine Square and so on, was a tightly packed community of working-class people. Their small homes were clustered around many alleyways and small streets with their own shops and pubs. A model, now preserved in Woodspring Museum, shows the scheme as originally planned with the area occupied by a tower block hotel, new library, shops and multi-storey car park. In the event funding was not forthcoming and, although the area was cleared and the people re-housed, none of the original scheme was built. The site was eventually developed with the Dolphin Square shopping precinct. Carlton Street car-park occupies the remainder of the site.

One major casualty of the war was Weston Airport. The entire Western Airways fleet had been requisitioned in 1940 and the business was never to regain its pre-war profitability. After several years of use by light aircraft and gliders the airport closed in the early 1980s.

The Second World War had brought new industries to Weston, chief among them aircraft production. After the war ended, vacant wartime factories were available and the borough council promoted the area heavily as an ideal base for light industry. The remaining aircraft factories also sought alternative goods to produce. One firm, the Bristol Aeroplane Company, began manufacturing prefabricated aluminium bungalows to address the acute housing shortage. Later they moved over to larger buildings such as schools and hospitals, often exporting these structures worldwide.

By the late 1960s foreign holiday destinations had become easier and less expensive to reach. All British seaside resorts faced a period of decline and Weston was no exception.

In 1974 Local Government re-organisation resulted in the formation of the new county of Avon. Weston's borough council was abolished and the town became the seat of local government for the district of Woodspring. This area stretched north to the outskirts of Bristol and included the towns of Nailsea, Clevedon and Portishead.

At the time of writing the Government has reviewed this situation and has ruled that Woodspring should become a Unitary Authority with the name North West Somerset. Avon County will be no more and Weston-super-Mare will be back in the county it never left, at least in the hearts of its residents—Somerset.

The Future

The future looks promising. Today, though many things have changed, Weston retains much of its original charm. There are still the lines of limestone houses, the beautiful parks, the piers and of course the sands.

People are now more likely to take several short holidays a year and the town has adapted to meet those needs.

Weston is lucky among modern seaside resorts. Many initiatives have taken place in recent years to improve the surroundings and amenities, to carry the resort into the 21st century. These include the Sovereign Centre Shopping Arcade, and the Sea Life Centre due to open in 1995.

In 1993 *Turning the Tide*, a heritage and environment strategy for a seaside resort, was published by the English Tourist Board and the Civic Trust using Weston-super-Mare as a model. The Tourism and Development Action Plan (TDAP) was formed as a three-year partnership between the public and private sectors. Its brief was to produce recommendations to regenerate Weston-super-Mare as a leading family seaside resort. One of the key areas of action was the re-appraisal of the Victorian and Edwardian heritage of Weston with a view to reawakening interest and appreciation of it. The original programme finishes in 1995 but the sponsors have agreed to continue this successful partnership.

With these initiatives in place let us hope the future of Weston-super-Mare is bright.

Mr Pigot's Cottage near the Bristol Channel Somerset

1 Mr. Pigot's Cottage, *c.*1790. This is the oldest illustration of Weston-super-Mare found so far. It shows the Lord of the Manor's summer cottage, The Grove, on the left, with a small thatched cottage in the centre. The latter has long since disappeared. The Grove was later enlarged and became known as Grove House.

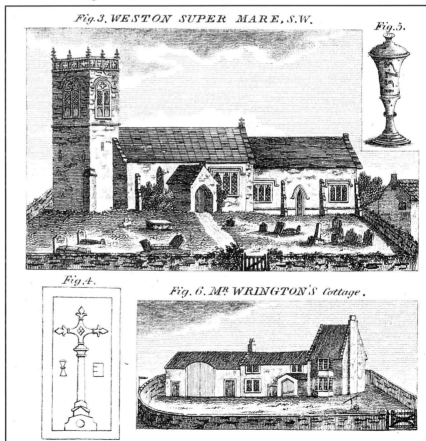

2 Weston parish church, 1805. This Norman church was demolished in 1824 and the present church built on the same site. The Tudor silver chalice was in use until the 1870s, after which date it disappeared. Below is the cottage built by the Rev. Leeves of Wrington. A part of this survives as the Old Thatched Cottage Restaurant.

3 Roger's Field, *c.*1842. On the left is *Reeve's Hotel*, the first hotel in Weston and now incorporated into the *Royal Hotel*. From the left the other buildings are South Parade, the High Street and Verandah House. This open space was known as Roger's Field after a later owner of *The Hotel*. It is now part of the Town Square.

4 Lower Church Road, *c.*1851. This print shows the new parish church built in 1824, with Churchill Cottage just in front, on what are now tennis courts. The National school, on the left, was built in 1845. It later became St John's School and is now the site of Weston College.

NATIONAL SCHOOL   ORIEL TERRACE   PARISH CHURCH

5 South Parade, *c.*1862. Christ Church, built in 1855, can just be glimpsed in the distance. The large building on the left is now the National Westminster Bank and has recently been restored. The iron railings, however, were all removed during the Second World War for salvage. The metal was used to build aircraft and bombs.

6 A general view of Weston-super-Mare from South Road, *c.*1864. Shrubbery Road is in the foreground. A train can just be seen centre left, on its way from Weston station to Weston Junction where the branch line joined the main Bristol and Exeter Railway line.

Parish Church.   Shrubbery Walk.   Royal Crescent.   The Sands.   Knightstone.

Brockley Crescent
Prince Consort Promenade Cliftonville

Wellington Terrace

Victoria Villas   Atlantic   Trinity Church   Atlantic Terrace
                   Terrace.   Weston Park

WESTON   SUPER   MARI

7 & 8   The two prints seen on this page join to form a panoramic view of the town, *c.*1867. This is a revised edition of the original print and has had several new buildings added, including Claremont Crescent and half of Atlantic Road. The new railway station, built in 1866, may be seen between the spires of Christ Church

Esplanade House   Royal   Rogers Hotel   High Street   Independent   Public   Regent St   Silverd Place
                  Terrace Cemetery   Montpelier Christ Church   Chapel   Library   Wesleyan Chapel

FROM   THE   SEA.

anilla Crescent   The Shrubbery Walks Princes Buildings   Albert Buildings   Park Place   Victoria Buildings   Parish   Lauriston
                            Knightstone   Royal Crescent   Church   Villas

ROM   THE   SEA.   No 1.

and Emmanuel Church. This was situated where Tesco now is and was the second of Weston's three main railway stations.

Lithographed by Norman & C.º 46 Watling St London

Church   Cambridge House   Portland   Marine   Belvidere   Walliscote   Dudley   Fern Villas   Holbrook Atlantic
                        Place   Villas   Ellenborough Crescent Villa   Ellenborough Park   House House

9 Claremont Crescent under construction, 1866. The little turreted, ivy-clad building on the headland was built in 1829. Known as Claremont Summer House, Frederick Martill opened it as a refreshment room in the 1840s.

10 Prince Consort Gardens. These were named in honour of Queen Victoria's dead husband. What is now the *Royal Pier Hotel* was then *Fenner's Hotel*. Below the hotel may be seen the remains of Claremont Bathing House, Weston's original bathing accommodation before Knightstone was developed. On the right is another view of Claremont Summer House.

11 Glentworth Bay, *c.*1870. This gives an idea of what the natural beach at Weston looked like before the promenades and sea wall were built. On the left are the impressive houses of Birnbeck Road and, on the right, Knightstone Baths.

12 Knightstone Baths and Harbour, *c.*1880. The building on the left is Dr. Fox's bath house, built in 1832. Dr. Fox took over Knightstone in 1830 with the intention of using sea water therapies in his pioneering treatment of the insane. The right-hand building was known as Arthur's Tower, and was a lodging house and reading room for the invalids.

13 *(above)* Birnbeck Pier, *c.*1870. This photograph shows the pier shortly after its opening in 1867. There is no steamer jetty to the north, but a short extension continuing on the line of the pier. The planks have been laid widthways in this view although later pictures show the planking laid lengthwise.

14 *(above right)* Birnbeck piermaster and one of his staff attend a steamer passenger and his luggage, *c.*1890. The pier toll house is in the background.

15 *(right)* A view landward from Birnbeck Pier, *c.*1900. The rocky walls of Worlebury Iron-Age hillfort can just be seen on the hilltop to the left. It is interesting to note the sparsity of trees at this end of the hill.

16 Knightstone Road, *c*.1870. The hut on the left is a cabman's rest. These were places for the drivers of the wagonettes and carriages to shelter from bad weather and have a brew. The cabbies were often the subject of complaint by local residents due to their exuberance and bad language.

17 The Promenade, *c*.1880. This shows the 1826 promenade, a flat walkway with no parapet. It was replaced in 1883 with the two-mile promenade still in use today. Here, the only amusements on the sands are some swingboats and donkeys, although there were more further south, including a rifle-shooting booth and concert parties.

18 Knightstone Road looking east, *c*.1885. The new promenade may be seen on the right. Albert Buildings, the elegant terrace on the left, is unrecognisable today. All these buildings are now hotels and extra storeys and front extensions have been added. The gardens have given way to forecourts.

19 Royal Terrace, *c*.1890. The garden in the foreground is that of the *Royal Hotel,* and was used an a tennis court for some years. Knightstone Island can be glimpsed in the distance to the left.

20   Anchor Head, *c.*1890. Once the ladies' bathing place, presided over by the brisk dipper, Betty Muggleworth, this sheltered beach is still a popular sun trap in summer. Betty would spread an old sail across the rocks behind which ladies would change into bathing dresses. Not everyone appreciated the service, however. Mrs. Rose Roberts wrote to her husband in Bristol in 1817, 'I drink the salt water in the morning, but do not bathe, being fearful of venturing my delicate frame out amongst the waves ... The gowns they make use of are such nasty looking things I do not think I could put one of them on.'

21 Anchor Head slipway, 1894. The boats are flatners, probably better known for trips round the bay than their winter use for fishing in the shallow waters round the coast.

22 Stow nets at Birnbeck, *c.*1894. The Birnbeck Fishery comprised several hangs of stow nets. These nets had a square mouth narrowing to a point at the back and were hung from two stakes driven into the mud thereby trapping fish on the ebbing tide. The catch, mostly sprats, was then collected at low tide.

23 A flatner in Weston Bay, *c.*1880, viewed from Knightstone. This photograph shows Weston seafront from the *Sandringham Hotel* to the College, now the *Grand Atlantic Hotel* (*see* no.124).

24 Weston sands, *c.*1870. Tayler's Bazaar stood on the corner of Regent Street. Once Whereat's Library and Reading Room, much of this building has been incorporated into the *Beach Hotel*.

25 Sand sculpture on Weston beach. Weston was one of the few coastal resorts with the right quality of sand for this activity. The largest set pieces took about eight days to complete but could last up to three weeks as long as they were above the tideline. A sand sculptor still worked on Weymouth beach until the 1980s.

26 Handbell ringers on Weston sands, 1893. This is just one example of the myriad of entertainment that took place on the beach. This would have included concert parties, donkey rides, photo booths, stalls selling refreshments and souvenirs, Punch and Judy shows, musicians and lots more.

27 Flatners under Birnbeck Pier, *c*.1918. Gangplanks have been laid to the boats so people do not get their feet too wet. This photograph shows the waterchute on the pier, which was built in 1905 and continued in use until 1931. The lifeboat house, built in 1902, is on the left.

28 Weston sands, *c*.1933. The platforms to the pleasure boats prevented people getting wet feet in the shallow water. Many beach stalls can be seen here and the tall building on the skyline is the *Grand Atlantic Hotel*.

29 Weston lifeboat *Colonel Stock*. Mrs. Anna Stock of Weston left a legacy of £4,888 to the RNLI which was used to purchase a new lifeboat and build a new lifeboat house on the south side of Birnbeck Pier. This is still in use today. The *Colonel Stock* served Weston from 1903 until 1933, saving 12 lives during this period.

30 The official naming ceremony of the lifeboat *Fifi & Charles* by the Duke of Kent, 27 June 1935. A group of ladies caused consternation by raising their dresses as the tide came in, in full view of the duke! This boat served Weston until 1962. During her service years she was launched 68 times, saving 83 lives. Many of these launches were during the Second World War, usually to search for survivors from crashed aircraft.

31 Building the Grand Pier, 1903. This pier was built at the end of Regent Street in an attempt to lure trippers into the centre of the town. Steamer passengers disembarking at Birnbeck Pier often got no further, spending the day on the amusements and in the bars and tearooms.

32 The interior of the Grand Pier Pavilion with the stagehands posing on the stage, *c*.1910. Judging by their paint-spattered clothing, the men here may well have just painted the backdrop in this photograph.

33 The Grand Pier, *c.*1915. On 16 May 1907 a further span of 450m, visible in this picture, was opened in order to allow steamers to berth. However, the tidal currents made this too dangerous and, after six attempts, the boat companies refused to call. It was dismantled in 1916.

34 The Grand Pier, *c.*1938. The greatest enemy of piers is fire and the Grand Pier was no exception. On the night of 13 January 1930 the pavilion was destroyed. Luckily, as it was at night, no one was hurt. After much discussion on whether to rebuild the pavilion in the same place or at the shore end, it was rebuilt in the same position and opened in 1933. The largest on any pier, the pavilion now houses a funfair instead of a theatre.

35 Gale damage, 10 September 1903. High tides and strong winds caused dramatic damage to the town and went down in history as the Great Gale. Here the bathing machines lie wrecked on the sea wall. They were already becoming old-fashioned and were therefore never replaced.

36 More gale damage as the flatner *Diamond Jubilee* lies across the tram tracks in Knightstone Road. A local trader, Mr. Bryant, was killed attempting to rescue people trapped in Knightstone Theatre.

37 Gale damage, 13 December 1981. A set of similar circumstances, that is, gale force westerly winds and a high tide, caused similar damage nearly eighty years later. Here the promenade wall was wrecked.

38 Gale damage to the Marine Lake colonnade, 1981. It was decided not to repair this damage but to demolish instead. Most seafront properties were flooded, the devastation seemingly even worse so close to Christmas.

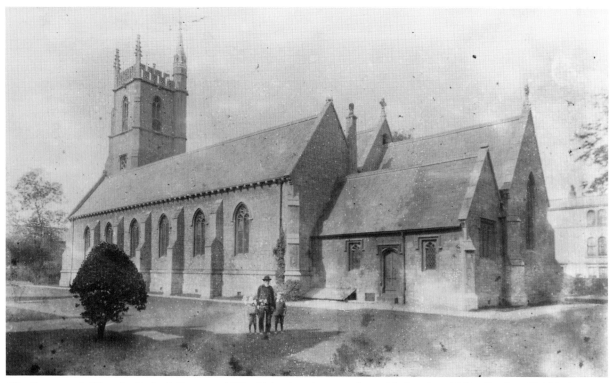

39 Emmanuel Church, Oxford Street, *c.*1871. This church opened on 15 October 1847. Costing £3,200, it was constructed by local builder, Robert Gregory. It is notable for a fine font in the form of an angel holding a shallow bowl, installed in 1920.

40 St Saviour's Church, Locking Road, opened on 28 August 1892. It was designed by local architect Sidney Wilde. This Sale of Work was held in 1904 to raise funds to help pay off a debt of £1,600 on the building fund.

St. Saviour's Church,

Weston-s-Mare.

An Interesting Event.

Our

Sale of

Work,

Victoria Hall,

June, 14, 15, 16,

1904.

41 St Joseph's Roman Catholic Church, *c*.1893. Opened in 1858, and built on land donated by Joseph Ruscombe Poole, it was the first Roman Catholic church in Weston. It attracted much anti-Catholic sentiment at the time, including an assault on the lord of the manor's pew in St John's Church, as he donated the building stone.

42 The Boulevard Congregational Church, *c*.1870. This church was destroyed by enemy action in 1942. A modern church was opened in 1959, built on the original foundations.

43 The Boulevard, 1887. In this view, construction is under way on no.51. The lane crossing the centre of this picture is Meadow Lane, now Baker Street. The field in front, now the site of the library and telephone exchange, was then often used for sick and injured animals.

44 The Boulevard and Waterloo Street looking west, 1888. At the end of the road is the *Royal Hotel*; the tower is part of the offices of the *Weston Mercury* newspaper (*see* no.94). This was just one of the many local buildings designed by local architect Hans Price and built in 1885. It is said to have been inspired by Price's visit to the Cathedral of Saragossa in Spain.

45 South Road from Grove Park Road. This is the most northerly road in Weston, developed in the 1850s. These snow-covered fields have long since been developed with Grove Park and Queens Roads.

46 Atlantic Road, c.1890. This area of town was mostly occupied by the upper middle classes. Eastern Mansions, the building with the fine ironwork balconies, was the childhood home of the actor John Cleese.

47 Shrubbery Lodge, 1918. This was one of three lodges guarding the entrances to the Shrubbery. This was a private estate centering on Villa Rosa, an Italianate mansion built in the 1830s for the Misses Pank. Standing on the junction of Shrubbery and Upper Church Roads, this lodge is the only one left today.

The Shrubbery, Westo...

48 The Shrubbery, *c.*1910. Most of the houses in the estate had access to areas of grass. Here a tennis net has been erected on the left. The turreted building is the Shrubbery Water Tower, which once supplied the water to Villa Rosa. The Tower has survived and is now a private residence. For many years it was the home of Peggy Nisbet. Mrs. Nisbet set up a local industry making costume dolls, now collected all over the world.

49 Glebe House, *c.*1900. Parts of this house were built in the 17th century. In 1644 the Royalist rector, Christopher Sadbury, imprisoned rebel villagers in the house. A new rectory was built in 1889 and Glebe House was sold. It has now been converted to privately owned flats.

·The Lodge
·Weston-super-Mare·

50 The Lodge, Bristol Road, 1914. Built for the 8th Earl of Cavan in 1863, this mansion was demolished in 1977, although the stable block remains. A housing estate covers the rest of the land.

51 Upper Bristol Road, *c.*1890. A view looking east with the cemetery lodge on the right. The land on the left of the road belonged to The Lodge (*see* no.50), but is now covered by a modern housing estate.

52 Grove Park Road, *c.*1894. A view of Weston that is not very different from one of today.

53 Ashcombe Park, *c.*1907. The land was purchased by the local authority in 1886 from the Capell family who owned Ashcombe House. In this photograph the avenue of lime trees have just been planted. In fact it is hard to recognise this viewpoint today.

54 This photograph shows the eastern entrance at the bottom of Grove Park. Much of this site is now occupied by a car park and public toilets. This area was once the scene of a minor riot when a charge was imposed for entry to the park!

55 Grove House, 1893. At this time the house was no longer in the ownership of the lord of the manor but housed Weston public library. The building suffered during two bombing raids and only the right-hand part in this picture is standing today. With a modern extension, it now serves as the Mayor's Parlour.

56 Another view of Grove House, Grove Park and the war memorial, 1937. At this time the house was a café.

57 A general view of Weston from Worlebury, 1900. In this photograph, the town has begun to spread, although there is little development south of the *Grand Atlantic Hotel.*

58 The junction of Southside and Victoria Quadrant, *c.*1900. The milk delivery cycle belonged to Minifie's Dairy, one of the largest dairies in the town with its own herds of dairy cattle.

59 Stafford Road, *c.*1920. One cannot help but wonder why trees were planted down the middle of the road itself, although they make a fine show here. Today, of course, they have all been felled.

60 No.11 Burlington Street, 1907. At the gate are Mrs. Alice Priddle and her family. This house is one of two properties built in 1864 by William Howlett; both are now owned by Woodspring Museum. This one provides office accommodation, whilst no.13 is Clara's Cottage, named after its owner, Clara Payne. It is displayed as a seaside landlady's home of 1900.

61 Hopkins Street looking towards Palmer Row. At the end of the road is the rear of Bryant & Sons, ironmonger's (*see* no.112). Hopkins Street is named after the Rev. Joseph Hopkins who owned the land.

62 Clifton Road, *c*.1910. Clifton Road comprised solid well-built Victorian villas for the middle classes. The cart belonged to Alfred Martin of Fore Street, Milton, grocer and provision dealer, no doubt on his daily delivery round.

63 Alfred Street, *c*.1910. At first glance little has changed here, only the details such as street furniture and traffic. However, today no one would stand in the middle of this busy road and stare, as some children are doing here.

64 Milton Brow, 14 April 1928. This picture shows these council houses shortly after construction. Following Addison's Act of 1919, Weston UDC was the first local authority in the country to provide public housing. This was at Milton Green.

65 Upper Bristol Road, Milton. The *Windsor Castle* pub on the left seems to have escaped from this major flood, *c.*1925. The *Windsor Castle* is one of the area's oldest inns and was once owned by George Sprake who built much of old Milton.

Upper Bristol Road, Milton. 1963.

The new

AND BETTER HOMES

A FEW HUNDRED YARDS FROM THE SEA

Joys

ASHCOMBE HOUSE ESTATE

WESTON-SUPER-MARE   *In the Centre of the Town*

Copyright by H. C. Joy]

66 Advertising brochure for the Ashcombe House Estate. These houses are in Milton Road, between the cemetery and Manor Road and included The Drive. Thirty-six plots were available and cost from £750. The drawing rooms were advertised with a 'handsome tiled surround with modern barless grate and a magnificent solid mahogany overmantel. An electric plug-in point is provided, for wireless.'

67 Weston General Hospital, 1908. This is the original hospital in Alfred Street, opened in 1865. You can just glimpse the sculpture of the Good Samaritan over the main door. This was carved by local sculptor Charles Summers, who later moved to Rome and gained an international reputation.

68 Bath night at the Children's Convalescent Home. This home was set up mainly for convalescing patients from the Bristol Children's Hospital. However, children from other such hospitals were also taken, as well as 'delicate children from private families' as long as space was available. It was on the corner of Clifton and Walliscote Roads.

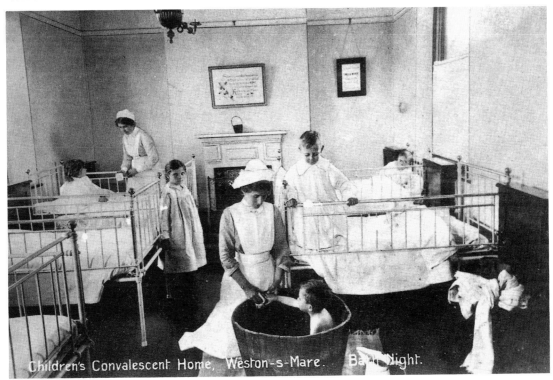

69   Weston Town Hall, *c.*1905. The original part of the building was completed in 1856 on land donated to the town by Henry Davies. It was substantially enlarged in 1897 with a further modern extension being opened in 1980.

70 The first railway station, 1846. Designed by Brunel, this station was a terminus at the end of a single track line from Weston Junction. It was situated where the Floral Clock is now. For many years the trains were drawn by horses in order to avoid having 'noisy, smelly' steam engines in the centre of the growing resort.

71 Weston railway station, *c.*1900. In 1866 a larger terminus was built, in turn superseded by this, the town's third and present station. It was built on a loop line into the town, so main line trains could at last call at Weston-super-Mare.

72 Drove Road railway bridge in the 1920s. This was one of four new railway bridges built when the loop line was opened to Weston station in 1884. They were all brick built with stone facings. Here work is taking place on widening the bridge to take increased road traffic.

73 The Weston, Clevedon & Portishead Light Railway station. Situated at the junction of Milton and Ashcombe Roads, this station was the terminus for this railway. Providing the only direct link between the three resorts, the line opened in 1897 and closed in 1938.

74 Donkey chair in Beach Road. These vehicles were used at Weston from the 1840s until the 1920s.

75 The *Waggon & Horses* inn. This inn, situated behind the *Victoria Hotel* (*see* no.127) in Regent Street, was the base for Vowles and Sons livery stables and carriage owners. In the 1870s the landlord's wife 'absconded with a lodger and all the silver'. Neither this inn nor the *Victoria Hotel* survives today.

76 Tram in Beach Road, *c.* 1930. The tram lines were laid in 1902, the route covering the sea front from the Sanatorium to Birnbeck Pier and inland along Oxford Street and Locking Road to the depot. The bus stop sign in the foreground is a sign of the competition that signalled the end of the trams in 1937.

77 Weston tram depot. This was built in Locking Road next to the Electricity Supply Company Works, opposite what is now Birchwood Avenue.

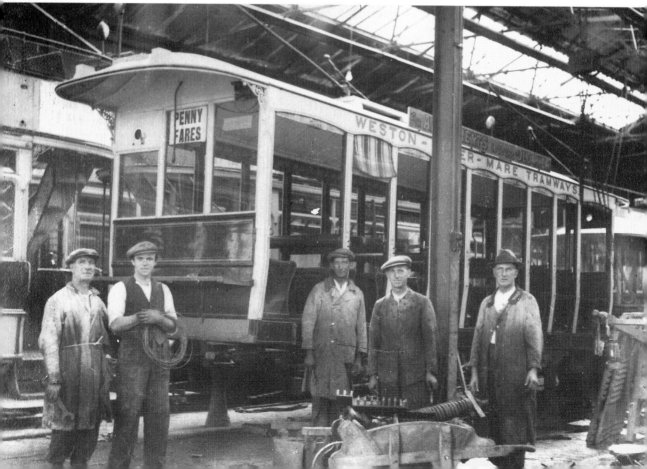

SEE THE BEAUTY
OF THE
WEST COUNTRIE
FROM A

COACH OR BUS

Off for a delightful tour through Somerset

Regular daily Bus Services (and Coach Tours during the summer) serve all the beauty spots, seaside resorts, and places of interest in the West Countrie.

Programme of Coach Tours and Timetable of Bus Services will be sent post free to any address on request.

● All Bus Services and Coach Tours start from BEACH GARAGE AND BUS STATION. This is also the Booking Office and Starting Point for Express Coach Services to all parts of the country; and Booking Office for Air Services to Birmingham, Bristol, Cardiff, etc.

> SALOON BUSES AND MOTOR COACHES ARE ALWAYS AVAILABLE FOR PRIVATE HIRE BY PARTIES

Address all Road and Air Travel enquiries to:

BRISTOL TRAMWAYS & CARRIAGE CO. LTD.
BEACH GARAGE AND BUS STATION, WESTON-SUPER-MARE
Telephone 110

Chief Offices at Bristol. Other Branches at Bath, Cheltenham, Coleford, Gloucester, Highbridge, Swindon and Wells

BEACH GARAGE. Accommodation for 600 Private Cars. Open day and night. Official Repairers to R.A.C.

78 Advertisement, 1937. This shows the Beach Road bus station, demolished in 1988 to make way for Carlton Mansions.

79 Locking Road, 1888. Road surfacing taking place outside the Royal Potteries. Established in the 1840s, this pottery built up a world-wide reputation for quality garden ornaments, as well as manufacturing bricks, tiles and flower pots. In the 1890s the firm moved to a new site in Langford Road, finally closing in 1961.

80 Surfacing the Melrose car park. The 1934 Bedford lorry was owned by Huish's Quarry of Worle. Second from the left is R. Durston.

81 Hillman's Foundry, Richmond Street. This foundry was responsible for much of the cast-iron street furniture in Weston. *Danesbury House*, fronting the foundry, is advertising Board Residence and Apartments to let. It is now a restaurant though the foundry closed in the 1960s.

82 Weston-super-Mare Gaslight Company's Workshops and Stores, Burlington Street, 1937. Built in 1912, the architect, William Jane, incorporated an existing stable yard. Now housing Woodspring Museum, the stable yard survives as the central courtyard feature.

83 Weston gas works, June 1928. At the top of the picture, in the centre, is the abattoir, recently demolished. The road crossing the picture diagonally is now Winterstoke Road and was the track of the railway branch line to Weston Junction.

84 Bringing ashore Weston's third Atlantic cable, 1901. These cables were submarine communication cables linking Britain with America.

85 Interior of the Atlantic cable office, 1929. This was on the seafront corner of Richmond Street. This communications link was of national importance and received a 24-hour guard during both world wars.

86 Post office vehicles and staff, *c.*1930. They are outside what was Weston's main post office from 1900 until the 1980s when it was demolished to make way for the Sovereign Centre.

87 Weston telephone exchange at the main post office, 1928. The supervisor, standing, is Miss Florence Horsington.

88 Hazelhurst Collegiate School for Girls, *c.*1909. This house was built in the 1840s as Glentworth Hall. It held an imposing position on Weston seafront where Glentworth Flats are now.

89 Pupils and staff of Stanmore House School for Girls, Royal Crescent, *c.*1905. This school, founded in 1848, was just one of many private schools in Weston. Around this time it was very fashionable to send children to seaside boarding schools and Stanmore House made much of its 'Particularly healthy and central situation' in its prospectus.

90 The Board schools, now Walliscote school, built in 1897. This was a Hans Price designed building, described as one of the finest Board Schools in England. A school board was established in Weston in 1894, to provide for public secondary education, which did not exist before this date.

91 Central Boys School; the woodwork class, *c*.1925.

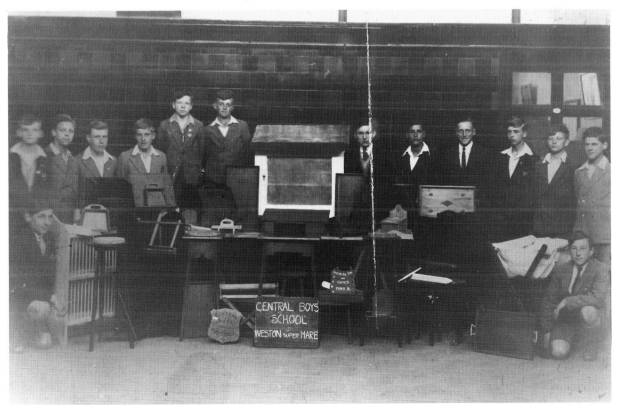

92 The National school, *c*.1880. This was on the corner of Knightstone Road and Lower Church Road where Weston College is now. The picture predates the building of the School of Science and Art, the end of Oriel Terrace being visible on the right.

93 School of Science and Art, *c*.1934. Opened in the 1890s, this is an example of the work of Hans Price, Weston's leading architect of that period. The building appears little changed today, although the south wing has been demolished.

94 Weston Mercury Office, Waterloo Street, 22 June 1897. This display won First Prize for Queen Victoria's diamond jubilee illuminations in the town. The original caption to the photograph records that: 'Nearly 600 Fairy Lamps, 100 Flags, Pennons and Bannerets—together with a quantity of Tricoloured Art Muslin and Transparencies, were utilised in the above Decoration'.

95 St James Street, decorated for the diamond jubilee of Queen Victoria, 1897. In the mid-19th century this was Weston's 'red light' district.

96 West Street, 1897. This street would be hard to identify today were it not for the distinctive carved heads of a goat and cow over Young's butcher's shop. These are still visible today.

97 Orchard Street, 1911. This view shows the street decorated for the coronation of George V.

98 Regent Street, 1911. More coronation decorations, on the shops of Lewis Wing, chemist, and the Misses Phillput, stationers.

99 Waterloo Street. This building is the Imperial Fire Office. Now the showrooms of the South Western Electricity Company, the crown on the roof is still there today.

100 Carlton Street area. This shows one of the many small backstreets in this part of Weston, decorated for the coronation of King George VI, 1937.

101 Milton Brow, 12 May 1937. This street party was to celebrate the coronation of King George VI.

102 Another view of St James Street, this time decorated for the coronation of Queen Elizabeth II, 1953. The child in the road is Pat Pople outside her father's shop.

103 High Street looking north, *c*.1905. On the left, two fine gas lamps mark the entrance to Post Office Road.

104   Locking Road, *c.*1917. In 1845 this area was known as New Town or Camden Town, and was home to the men who were building Weston. In this view a crowd has gathered outside Mr. Bishop's butcher's shop. As this was wartime, and meat was rationed, it may be that some supplies had just arrived.

105   Dumfries Place, Tuesday 14 March 1938. W. Cousins and L. Trowbridge of the Bristol Co-op Society with their horse, Boxer.

106   18 Meadow Street, *c*.1893. Knott's Central Stores with Mr. Knott third from left. The man wearing the hat is a travelling salesman.

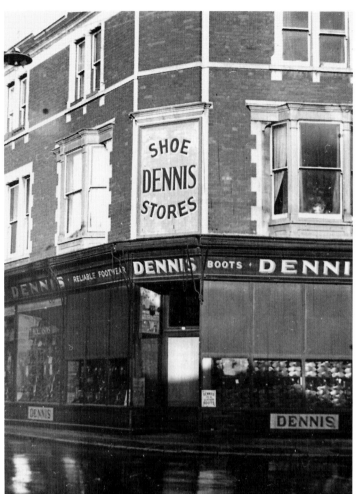

107 Dennis' shoe shop. This was on the corner of Meadow Street and Orchard Street. The shop is still recognisable today, although it currently stands empty.

108 High Street from Post Office Road, *c.*1890. Coulsting's Bazaar later opened a café on the first floor. It was a very long narrow shop which induced a great sense of exploration. It still existed in the 1970s and I well remember its wonderful atmosphere.

109 A wrapping paper with advert for Mr. Willett's shop, *c*.1900.

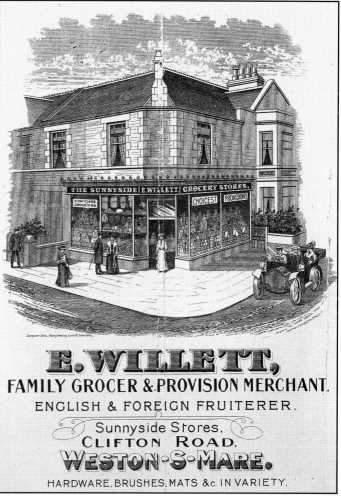

110 Lance & Lance department store. This well-known shop stood on the corner of Waterloo Street and High Street. It took a direct hit from incendiary bombs during the Second World War and was totally demolished. Even today, locals still refer to this as Lances' Corner, to the confusion of 'newcomers'.

111 High Street, *c*.1890. Fox and Mackie later became Leaver & Fox. They are still operating today, as Leaver's, in premises in Waterloo Street. An interesting selection of goods can be seen on sale here including garden seats and rollers, a fire grate, gas lamps, food covers, coal scuttles and pumps.

112 The Boulevard, *c*.1900. This picture is of another local ironmonger, Bryant and Sons. Again an interesting range of goods is displayed, from pushchairs to spades, bicycles to knives.

113 High Street, *c.*1900. Mr. Coles' Christmas display of poultry. This shop was situated in the High Street, now the site of the Tudor Shopping Mall. The alley on the left leads to the *Britannia Inn*.

A SAFE and EFFECTUAL CURE for Spinal Affections, Rheumatism, Lumbago, Chilblains, Bronchocele, Swelling of the Glands, Weakness of Joints, Sprains, Bruises, Tumours, &c.

GIBBONS' ESSENCE OF SEAWEED

The Pier, Weston-Super-Mare.

114 Label for Gibbons' Essence of Seaweed. Mr. Gibbons ran chemist shops in Upper Church Road and West Street, from 1861 until 1887.

115 The interior of Widgery's chemist shop, West Street, March 1968. Most of the contents and fittings were donated to Woodspring Museum when the shop was modernised shortly after this photograph was taken.

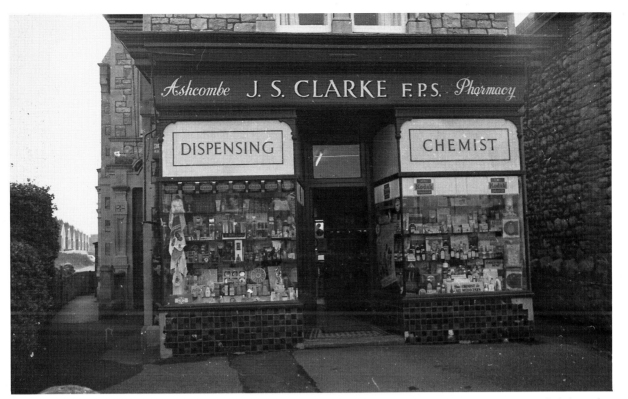

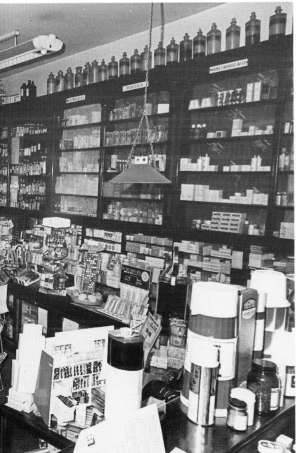

116 Ashcombe Pharmacy, on the corner of Ashcombe Road and Milton Road, 1984. This building was once the station master's house for the Weston, Clevedon & Portishead Light Railway, the Weston terminus for which was just up the alley to the left.

117 Barnett's radio and cycle shop on the corner of Baker Street and Alfred Street, 1930s. This was a great period for entertainment in Weston, with posters for three local cinemas and theatres on this hoarding.

118 Freeman, Hardy and Willis' shoe shop, High Street, 12 September 1950.

CENTRE OF HIGH STREET

Telephone **70**

QUALITY

SERVICE

A LOCAL INDUSTRY

CATERING—

Birthday, Wedding and Christening Cakes

Gateaux

Chocolates

Toffees

Boiled Sugars

Marzipan Fruits

Bath Buns

Cream Buns

Chocolate Eclairs

Meringues

Creams

Trifles

Jellies in variety

MADE ON THE PREMISES

MORNING COFFEE A SPECIALITY

Excellent Special Accommodation for small or large parties in addition to the Cafe

- **ORANGE ROOM**   seating about **40** persons
- **GREEN ROOM**   seating about **100** persons

     and with alternative entrance from North Street

- **QUEEN'S HALL**   seating about **200** persons
- **KING ALFRED HALL**   seating about **200** persons

FOR BOOKINGS AND SUGGESTED MENUS APPLY MANAGERESS

119 An advertisement for Brown's Café, taken from the town guide for 1937. This popular eating place had a bakery on the ground floor as well as a restaurant, function rooms and a roof garden. This building was demolished in 1994.

120 The Central Café in the Royal Arcade, *c.*1930. The arcade was built in 1891 and provided a covered shopping area with entrances in Post Office Road, Regent Street and Salisbury Terrace. The major part of it was demolished in the 1940s.

121 The interior of the Central Café with the staff on the left, *c.*1930.

122 An invoice from George Phillips of 1 Elizabethan Villas, to Mr. Hayman for accommodation, April 1900. Notice the interesting range of facilities including 'Hire of Bath', 'Fires' and 'Gas'.

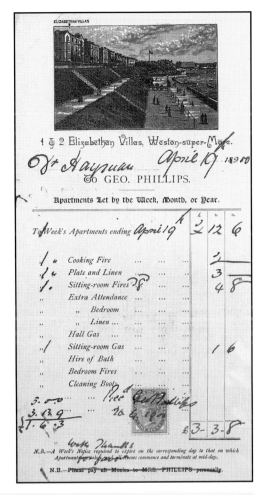

123 The *Seaward Hotel*, 46 Knightstone Road, c.1928. This building is still run as the *Seaward Hotel*, although the building has been greatly altered in appearance.

124 The *Grand Atlantic Hotel, c.*1890. Built as a school in 1854, this building was converted into a hotel in 1889. It was named after the Atlantic cable, an undersea communications cable which came ashore in front of this hotel (*see* no.84).

125 A bedroom at the *Grand Atlantic Hotel, c.*1928. The tariff at this time was from 14s. 6d. per day for a double room, 8s. 6d. per day for a single room and 10s. 6d. for a sitting room. A fire in the bedroom cost 4s. per day extra.

126 The ballroom of the *Grand Atlantic Hotel, c.*1928. This was replaced in the 1930s with a wonderful Art Deco style ballroom which would not have been out of place on an ocean liner and is still used today.

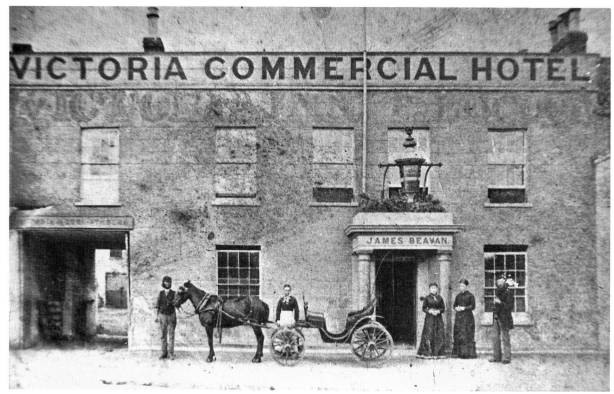

127 The *Victoria Commercial Hotel, c.*1880. This was one of Weston's oldest inns and was situated in Regent Street, where the main post office is now.

128 Shop on the corner of Orchard Place and Meadow Street after a fire, 1930s. The building was refurbished and may still be seen today.

129 Huntley's Restaurant, High Street, 25 May 1904. It is seen here after the tragic fire in which six people died, four of them members of the Huntley family. The whole town mourned on the day of the funeral and crowds lined the route of the cortège. The pulpit in the parish church is a memorial to two of the victims.

130 Cartoon by the famous local cartoonist, Alfred Leete. It is mocking an event in Weston during the First World War, when someone reported seeing a German U-boat off Glentworth Bay!

131 Troops digging a demonstration trench on Weston beach. The first draft of Kitchener's army was billeted at Weston during the winter of 1914-15. These soldiers suffered terrible losses in France, just 10 days after leaving Weston.

132 Troops training in Clarence Park, *c*.1914. Equipment was limited and broom handles were used in place of rifles.

133 Medical aid soldiers at Weston station on their way to France.

134 During the First World War, Ashcombe House, at the top of The Drive, was commandeered as a Red Cross convalescent hospital for wounded soldiers. These two men are holding collecting boxes for the Red Cross.

135 Convalescent soldiers with a nurse at Ashcombe House Red Cross Hospital.

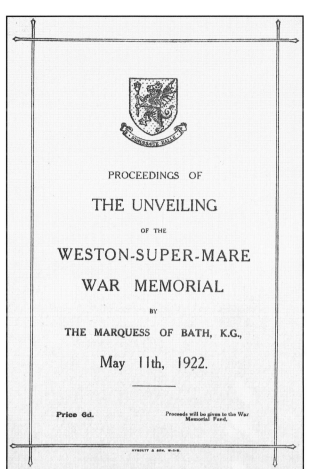

PROCEEDINGS OF

THE UNVEILING

OF THE

WESTON-SUPER-MARE

WAR MEMORIAL

BY

THE MARQUESS OF BATH, K.G.,

May 11th, 1922.

Price 6d.

Proceeds will be given to the War
Memorial Fund.

HYSSETT & SON, W.-S-M.

136 The cover of a programme for the unveiling ceremony of the war memorial in Grove Park, 1922. The unveiling itself was performed by the Lord Lieutenant of Somerset, the Marquess of Bath, with the dedication by the Bishop of Bath and Wells. Mogg's Military Prize Band played the accompaniment to the hymns.

137 The war memorial, Grove Park. The sculptor was Alfred Drury R.A. It was erected in memory of the men of Weston, Uphill and Kewstoke who fell in the First World War; 380 names are inscribed on its panels.

138 St Paul's Church, Walliscote Road, after Weston's first major blitz in January 1941. It continued to be used, with services held in the south aisle or in the church hall in Walliscote Road. After the war it was repaired and reconsecrated in 1957.

139 During the Second World War large numbers of American troops were billeted in Weston for the run up to D-Day. Here 'Blackie', Oscar and Lee Mullins pose outside their billet at 115 Severn Road, Weston, 1944.

140 The Weston-super-Mare Auxiliary Fire Brigade, 1939-45.

141 The switchback on Birnbeck Pier. This was just one of many popular amusements offered on the pier, including a helter skelter, waterchute and bioscope.

142 Flying machine, another of the amusements on Birnbeck Pier, *c*.1909.

143 The interior of Knightstone Baths, *c.*1905. Opened in 1902, this pool was Weston's only indoor swimming facility until the 1980s when the new pool at Hutton Moor was built. This photograph was taken by Walter J. Davies.

144 Roller skaters at the Skating Rink, Bristol Road, 8 August 1909. Roller skating was extremely popular at the turn of the century and Weston boasted three rinks, this one on the corner of Worthy Place, the Tivoli in the Boulevard and one on Birnbeck Pier. In addition there were special afternoons for roller skating on the Grand Pier.

145 Winner of the prize for Most Original Exhibit in the Weston Carnival, 14 November 1912. The November Carnivals are an old Somerset tradition. The series of carnivals takes place every year, starting with the Guy Fawkes Carnival at Bridgwater, and ending at Weston-super-Mare. Today they are illuminated spectaculars averaging over 100 floats.

146 The Bristol Tramways and Carriage Company float in Weston Carnival, 13 November 1930.

147 Weston Gas Company's carnival float, 1920s.

148 Another Bristol Tramways and Carriage Company float featuring HMS *Weston* and entered in the 1934 carnival. Among those pictured are Messrs. L. Hawkins, A. Scrivian, B. Denmead, B. Attwell, R. Reed, S. Lang, -?- Burrows, J. Moore, S. Jones, K. Burnell, F. Hooper and B. King.

LILY POND, WINTER GARDENS, WESTON-SUPER-MARE.

149 Construction underway on the Winter Gardens Pavilion, Tuesday 14 September 1926. Due to covenants on the land which restricted the height of buildings, the Pavilion ballroom was sunk to 137 cm below ground level.

150 The interior of the Winter Gardens Pavilion a few years after its opening. Aside from the furnishings, it is little changed today.

151 Installing a First World War Tank in Alexandra Parade, 1919. This was on the site of what is now the floral clock. It was placed there to celebrate local efforts on behalf of War Savings.

152 The floral clock, Alexandra Parade, 1962. This was constructed in 1935 as an attractive feature to replace the rusting tank. This design commemorated 25 years of Weston Borough.

153 *(top left)*   Workmen involved in building Marine Lake, 1927.

154 *(bottom left)*   Constructing the Marine Lake, completed in 1928. It was built to provide a part of the beach where the tide was always in, and which could be used for swimming, paddling and boating.

155 *(above)*   Another view of Marine Lake under construction, 1927.

156 Work in progress in building the open air pool. It was opened on 1 July 1937.

157 A view of the open air pool, 1 August 1960. The whole building was refurbished in 1983 and relaunched as The Tropicana leisure pool.

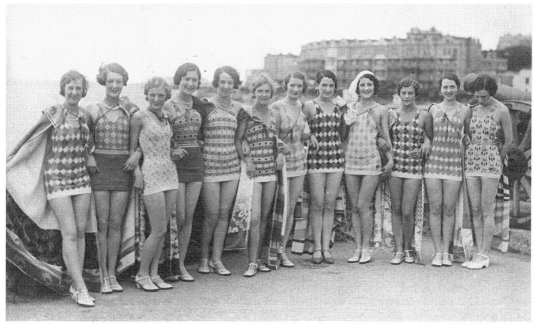

158 Beauty contest, 1932. Can you name any of these bathing beauties?

159 The famous Irish tenor, Joseph Locke, with the four winners in the third round of the Modern Venus beauty contest, 15 July 1954. This beauty contest was very popular, attracting many well-known people as judges, including Laurel and Hardy.

THE
CORNWALL AVIATION COMPANY,

This is to Certify that

B. G. Dood

Flew ~~on~~ and Looped

in an Avro Biplane at

Weston-Super-Mare.

on August 11th 1980.

PILOT.

160 *(top left)* Certificate showing that Mr. B. Wood flew in an Avro biplane, 1930.

161 *(bottom left)* An Avro biplane taking off from Weston sands, *c.*1930. In the early days of flying it was common for these small aircraft to take off from and land on the beach.

162 *(above)* Weston Airport, 1937 with the Western Airways fleet of aircraft.

163 The Regent Picture House, later the Gaumont cinema, in Regent Street, 1937. This whole site, including the garage next door, was cleared in the 1980s and Mr. B's Fun Factory built.

164 The Central Picture House in Oxford Street was another of Weston's several cinemas, 1937.

165 The Odeon cinema, 19 June 1954. The film showing, in addition to a film of the Queen's tour of Australia, was *Carnival Story*, advertised by a cut-out on the roof of a bathing girl.

166 Corner of High Street and Waterloo Street, 12 November 1954. At first glance this looks like yet another news placard. It is really advertising the film *Suddenly* at the Odeon! Note the extensive bomb damage to this part of town. The site of Lance & Lance's shop (*see* no.110), right, is being used as a temporary car park.

167 The interior of the Playhouse, 1950s. This was once the Market Hall in High Street, converted with seating and a hessian-draped ceiling. When it rained it is said that the performers could still smell the animals that were once sold here!

168 The Playhouse, May 1963. This is the same building as in the picture above but with further improvements. The building burned down in August 1964 and was replaced five years later with the modern purpose-built theatre enjoyed today.

169 The Centre, *c.*1935. This Art Deco style row of shops adjoined the new Odeon cinema (*see* no.165). A lot of the detailing has since been lost, including the rain canopy in places.

170 Another view of The Centre and the Victoria Methodist Church. This church was built in 1931 after fire destroyed the original Victorian one.

171 Carlton Street, 1957. The *Prince of Wales* pub and Salvation Army hall are still there today but most of the other buildings were demolished in the clearance of the late 1950s.

172 Oxford Street, *c*.1957. This was all part of the Carlton Street area clearance. It was originally planned to develop the whole area with a new hotel, shops, library, housing and parking. Funding never materialised, however, and a much smaller development took place, resulting in the Dolphin Square precinct.

173 Camden Cottage, Beach Road, *c.*1960. Built in the 1840s, this picturesque home was once owned by Samuel Pollitt as a summer cottage. Its last owner was the Rev. Israel Westhead. Rev. Westhead was curate of St Paul's Church in the 1920s. He later became rector at Temple Cloud and retired to Camden Cottage. It was demolished in the 1970s.

174 Little Britain. This model village was opened on 7 June 1962 by television personalities Armand and Michaela Denis, and councillor and Mrs. Moore. There were 42 different buildings, and more were added later. It was built on the seafront next to the Winter Gardens, on what is now part of the *Royal Hotel* car park. The village even featured on television in a programme on Weston by poet, Sir John Betjeman.

175 Marine Lake, 1950s.

176 Beach Road and the *Sandringham Hotel*, 1950s.

177 High Street, 9 February 1961. Construction can be seen taking place on the bombed site of Lance & Lance.

178   The Winter Gardens putting green and High Street, 20 July 1964. The putting green was removed in the 1980s for the Sovereign Centre and Town Square development. Note the one-way traffic in the High Street, now pedestrianised.

179 High Street South, with the Central cinema in Oxford Street, just before its demolition, 1964.

180 Dolphin Square, 23 January 1967. This shopping centre never really achieved its original aim of extending the shopping area away from the High Street.

181 Hovercraft on Weston sands, 5 August 1963. As the popularity of its paddlesteamers waned, P & A Campbell experimented with this hovercraft service between Weston and Penarth in Wales. Tickets cost £1, the 11-mile journey taking 12 minutes.